MW00445932

EMILIO PUCCI

First published in the United States of America in 1998
by UNIVERSE PUBLISHING
A Division of Rizzoli International Publications, Inc.
300 Park Avenue South
New York, NY 10010

and

THE VENDOME PRESS

©1998 Éditions Assouline, Paris
English translation copyright ©1998 Universe Publishing

Front cover photograph: Dress embroidered with beads and Svarowski
crystals on twill. Autumn/Winter collection 1966–1967.
© Emilio Pucci Archives/D.R.

Back cover photograph: Emilo Pucci surrounded by his models, for the
launch of the perfume "Vivara," in February 1966 in Acapulco.
© Photo: Toni Frissell/
Emilo Pucci Archives/D.R.

Text and captions translated by Elizabeth Currie

ISBN: 0-7893-0250-0

Printed and bound in Italy

Library of Congress Catalog Card Number: 98-61194

EMILIO PUCCI

BY MARIUCCA CASADIO

UNIVERSE / VENDOME

i t was during the sixties and seventies, years full of vitality and optimism and marked by an active confidence in progress, that Emilio Pucci's designs established their reputation and met with unconditional approval, becoming, as never before, a fashion phenomenon, the symbol of an era of good taste. It became an obligatory sign of distinction to wear his designs by day and by night, on vacation both at the seaside and in the mountains. They constituted a whole look that ranged from underwear and household linens to handbags, perfumes, and rugs. Pucci's creations began to touch the collective imagination.

At the beginning of this creative adventure, during the late forties and early fifties, the international fashion market had been entirely dependent on Parisian haute-couture designs. In America, where Pucci was received with the most gratifying and universal acclaim, women only wore models that were either original French creations or else inspired by them. Christian Dior's "New Look," which featured abundantly in *Vogue* and *Harper's Bazaar*, and collections by such designers as Givenchy, Balenciaga, Chanel, Fath, and Balmain imposed impeccably structured silhouettes, crafted down to the smallest details. Between 1947 and 1957 international attention centered on Dior, who was introducing at least two new lines a year. "Corolle" (Flared), "Envol" (Flight), "Ailée" (Winged), "Verticale," "Oblique," the famous "H" and "A" lines, as well as the "Trapèze" line (which marked Yves Saint Laurent's arrival at the fashion house), made him the absolute king of creativity.

At the same time, almost unnoticed, the United States developed a flourishing trade in sportswear as a response to the demands of modern American society, which appeared to have a great need for clothing that was simultaneously elegant, simple, and comfortable to wear. The birth of companies such as Clare McCardell, Tina Leser, and Tom Brigance gave casual wear a new legitimacy, refinement, distinction, and elegance. Their creations made use of the latest technology, but none of the companies possessed the vision or imagination that would transform taste and influence the market trend in an incisive and radical manner.

It appears that Emilio Pucci, who had studied at American universities and remained strongly attached to the country's culture, was the first person to understand and respond to this need. With his refined personality and natural elegance, this twentieth-century dandy, the marquis of Barsento, belonged to one of the oldest and most important families of the Italian aristocracy. Of Florentine descent, he was born in Naples, with Russian blood inherited from his father (his great-grandmother was a niece of Empress Catherine and his grandmother was linked by marriage to Peter the Great's family). Pucci grew up in the heart of Florence in a palazzo whose walls were decorated with paintings by Botticelli, Raphael, Donatello, and Leonardo da Vinci. But despite his ancestry, the young marquis appeared more in tune with the rhythms and lively pace of the present. He was a skilled and active member of modern society: a passionate and accomplished fencer, pilot, skier, swimmer, and tennis player, he also loved traveling. His career in fashion began almost by accident, while he was still a pilot officer in the Italian air force.

Emilio Pucci seemed to embody the synthesis between ancient and modern. The dangerous missions he undertook in the Italian air force during the Second World War showed him to be brave and bold. This fearlessness, when coupled with his charismatic and authoritarian elegance, gave him a singular personality that fascinated the transatlantic public. Journalists and writers from the United States supported him and his ideas unreservedly, in the certainty that the American public, with no aristocratic tradition of its own, would be unable to resist him. The market seemed to appreciate the aura that surrounded him as much as his creative talents. From the fifties onwards, people hurried to buy clothes designed by Pucci, granting him instant and universal success.

The radical nature of Pucci's style was in many ways the antithesis of French haute couture. It was an embodiment of freedom, confidence, and presence. His brightly colored, synthetic clothes emphasized physical exuberance as well as a feminine intellectual charisma. Intended to dress women for their everyday movements, to liberate them from the weight of costly and cumbersome wardrobes, and to accompany and facilitate their entry into the business world, Emilio Pucci's creations revolutionized the very concept of fashion. They formed an original fusion between sportswear and urbanwear, craft and industry, Italian style and American market demands. In a totally unforeseen manner, they became a fashion phenomenon, coveted and sought after on both sides of the Atlantic.

The energy that Pucci communicated through his bright colors; the originality of his painted, printed, or embroidered fabrics; the technical innovations he applied to materials; his eclectic rapport with existing fabrics, as well as his ability to experiment, made him the perfect spokesman for his time. He became a *sui generis* designer who would influence taste for more than half a century. If Parisian haute couture pursued objectives of formal perfection, of spectacular aesthetics, transforming the female body into an impeccably clothed, completely static image, then Pucci's designs eliminated weight, volume, and accumulations of layering to highlight instead the identity of the wearer. This constituted the beginnings of a concept which remains with us today. It is no coincidence that the marquis achieved his greatest fame during the sixties and seventies, when women were starting to play a more prominent role in social activities and in the business world. That Italian, French, and American ready-to-wear collections have recently paid tribute to Pucci's style confirms the modernity of the designer's intuitions. In the work of Gianni Versace, Karl Lagerfeld, Stephen Sprouse, and Jean-Paul Gaultier, it is often possible to detect traces of the ever-fashionable spirit of some of Pucci's most famous creations.

Whenever Pucci was asked why he had chosen to work in fashion, he invariably replied: "Because I like pretty women!" Nothing could have been more true. Right from the beginning, the Florentine had dedicated his energy to emphasizing beauty, which he believed emanated from both personality and a spirit of naturalness. Pucci loved looking at women. It was, moreover, thanks to one of his female friends that he embarked on a career in fashion. (His interest in his own image meant that he already designed garments for his personal wardrobe.) One day he showed a friend a skiing ensemble that he had designed—a pair of trousers fitting closely over ski boots with a band of leather passing under the sole of the foot; a sweater and a shirt; and an anorak designed like a parka, with a hood and a front pocket closed with a zipper at the belt. The photographer Toni Frissell, who regularly worked for *Harper's Bazaar*, expressed her enthusiasm for this ski outfit, which was so elegant and perfect for a woman's physique but not yet available on the market. She was the first person to convince Pucci to produce his designs industrially.

The photos Frissell took of this first ski outfit arrived a few days later on the desk of Diana Vreeland, the editor of *Harper's Bazaar* and one of the most powerful figures in the fashion world. Vreeland was later to become one of the most dedicated and influential promoters of Pucci's work. She published the photographs in the December 1948 issue in an article entitled "An Italian Skier Designs." In the meantime she contacted Marjorie Griswold, a buyer for the large department store Lord & Taylor on New York's Fifth Avenue, convinced that Pucci possessed all the necessary characteristics to break into the American market. The Spring/Summer collection of 1948, the first that Pucci designed for Lord & Taylor, contained a small group of garments, notably a two-piece ski suit in blue gabardine, a pair of ski pants in the same material, two men's shirts in cotton poplin, and three tunics in knitted wool. The exclusiveness of the design and fabric of the tunics, which were made with Capri wool, presented insurmountable problems when it came to manufacturing them on an industrial scale. Pucci, however, was undeterred. He didn't ever want to compromise the qualities of craftsmanship that were so integral to Italian culture, since he was convinced that they contributed to the appeal of his designs on the international market.

Pucci dispensed with girdles, linings, padding, petticoats, and all other superfluous undergarments. For Pucci, the essential aspects of modern clothing were simplicity (a combination of studied cuts and precise geometric forms); color (the use of exclusive materials, which, according to the season, were printed with abstract motifs in original colors, inspired by natural landscapes or exotic cultures); style (synonymous with beauty, expressed through clothing that camouflaged defects and exalted the qualities of the female body); and, finally, movement (the garments were intended for an active lifestyle, to be enhanced by the bearing and comportment of those who wore them). He sought to create a novel form of complicity between craft and industry, haute couture and sportswear, formal elegance and a casual wardrobe. Rooted in tradition, yet taking advantage of the possibilities offered by progress, he combined the feminine and masculine, fusing artistic evocation with poetic craftsmanship. These elements gave his style an indisputable originality, projecting it into the future, and, from the early fifties, Pucci ranked among the most promising designers on the Italian scene.

In 1948, at the time of his encounter with Diana Vreeland and of his first collection for Lord & Taylor, Emilio Pucci was thirty-three years old and still a pilot officer with the Italian air force. He had considerable economic difficulties and had not yet made the decision to abandon the air force for a career in fashion. Speaking of this period in an interview, Pucci declared that: "I have known difficult times and I am not ashamed to admit it. If I have succeeded at all in the world of fashion, it is thanks to my enthusiasm and my determination—I must have a will of iron." Nevertheless, his first successes, though modest, gave him a greater awareness of his own talent and allowed him to focus on his creative potential. He confided in his friend Toni Frissell: "At the moment I am working on a number of new ideas, which range from clothing to car models. I have already produced some designs, and am now concentrating on a collection of clothes for next summer." His capacity for reinterpreting what already existed became increasingly evident during the sixties. The aim of his work, as he himself defined it, was to put himself "at the service" of others and to improve different aspects of the quality of life, from clothing through to habitat.

P ucci designed his second summer collection in 1949 in Capri, the island that was to have such a strong influence on his sense of color and on the themes of his prints.

Taking advantage of a long period of leave, and with the pretext of designing some clothes for a friend, he created a series of garments, notably bathing suits, playing on the chromatic juxtaposition of black and white. Even though they were made by local craftsmen, who paid little attention to the finer details of the garments, they were immediately successful. Swiftly copied and worn by all the elegant residents of Capri, the models were seen at Portofino, on the Côte d'Azur, and along all the Mediterranean beaches. It was predominantly synthetic materials that were used for the collection, among them nylon and its derivatives—easy to maintain, resistant, and magically elastic—and helanca, which possessed even more amazing qualities (it can be stretched to up to five times its original length without losing its shape). Also, many pieces were made of jersey, produced by mixing wool and acetate-based synthetic fibers, which is often used in sportswear. Pucci's small collection centered around simple forms, with a youthful and functional spirit, intended to be worn throughout the whole day. It included white piqué jackets, short skirts with side splits, blue shorts, men's jackets, shirts to be worn over Capri pants, handwoven straw hats, open-toed sandals, white piqué sundresses for the day, or little silk tops combined with two-piece skirts tied at the sides for the evening.

the technical results achieved by the Florentine fashion house over the years—namely new dyes and the treatment of cottons and silks to obtain unbelievable qualities—would have been impossible without the involvement and close collaboration of the Italian textile industry. In 1948, for example, Pucci joined forces with Guido Ravasi, a silk industrialist. At the same time, Legler and Valle Susa were carrying out research for Pucci on cottons and their by-products. The interest that he aroused within the textile industry, a fundamental recognition in itself of his creative talent, filled Emilio Pucci with enthusiasm and gave him hope for future success. At the same time, Pucci also had his clothing produced in Capri, by small-scale tailors along the coast, not only because of the low production costs, but also because he adored spending his free time on the beautiful island. There, free from distractions, he was able to dedicate himself to completing his designs.

Therefore, the marquis created a style that was inextricably linked to his intellectual and aesthetic charisma. Capri never ceased to stimulate him: the azure of the Blue Grotto, the pink of the bougainvilleas, the green and yellow of the mimosas and wild plants, of the mints and lemons. . . . Quite rightly, it was this synthesis of authenticity and refinement that inspired his designs, the characteristics of which would become known as "Emilio style."

In 1950 Pucci decided to abandon his military career and open a boutique, La Canzone del Mare (The Song of the Sea), at Marina Piccola, a decision that provoked much curiosity and created a scandal among his aristocratic friends and relatives who considered work rather beneath their status. His daughter Laudomia recalls that he never lost his biting wit and found different ways to discourage their curiosity and tease them about their embarrassment: "He used to keep, for example, a bucket and brush behind the door. When someone he knew came into the boutique, he brought them out, got down on his hands and knees and began to wash the floor." Along with La Canzone del Mare was born a revolutionary label that belonged somewhere midway between American mass production and French haute couture. It applied to a small number of handmade garments—typified by their essential forms and sold at relatively reasonable prices—that were far removed from the type of fashion that was so successful in Paris and New York.

In order to please his followers, as well as the suppliers, Pucci opened his first workshop on the second floor of his palazzo. Here, the Prince of Prints, as he was later to be christened by the American press, lived with his wife and children. It was also the site of his future activities and subsequently became the drawing workshop, the firm's commercial headquarters, and also the venue for his shows. The new prints and collections were presented on the second floor, in the grandiose and evocative surroundings of the ballroom, triumphantly decorated with frescoes and baroque stuccos. As the careful spokesman for his style, Pucci knew how to integrate the ancient and modern, and marry his creations with the imposing presence of Roman busts and inlaid marble floors, frescoes, and old-master paintings. The press and buyers flocked there en masse, and waited with bated breath for the productions of this creative genius. Pucci was actively involved in the shows, finding the models, solving problems, and arranging last-minute accessories himself. Even though he defined himself as a craftsman, Emilio Pucci was, at heart, a forerunner of what we would now call a "style entrepreneur." He was in charge of the designs, the links with clients and suppliers, the running of the catwalk shows, the publicity and the photo shoots. He fulfilled the orders of important clients, such as Braniff International, a private Texan airline whose uniforms he created, and Ford, for whom he designed the interior and upholstery of the Lincoln Continental Mark IV in 1977.

a t the beginning of the fifties, Giovan Battista Giorgini played an important role in Pucci's career. As an organizer of the first fashion show in Florence, Giorgini found the Italian boutique collections so interesting that he included them in the opening program on February 12, 1951, which attracted only a handful of buyers and American journalists. Although Pucci was already the most famous of the thirteen fashion houses and boutiques invited, this show marked the start of his popularity with the American market and the intriguing potential of his designs from La Canzone del Mare was recognized. When the Italian catwalk shows moved to the Grand Hotel in Florence that July, Pucci became aware of the interest his work was generating. It was during this period that he met Stanley Marcus, of Neiman-Marcus in Dallas, who was enthusiastic about buying certain designs. This marked the beginning of Pucci's collaboration with the big department stores, such as Neiman-Marcus and later Saks Fifth Avenue, I. Magnin, and Bergdorf Goodman. Before long, "Emilio style" was available at the most important stores in the United States and, in 1954, Pucci won the Neiman-Marcus Award, presented annually to figures in the fashion world who are distinguished by their creativity and originality.

f ollowing in the footsteps of Coco Chanel, whose own style was also linked with the search for innovative fabrics, Pucci patented numerous original materials. The first of these was silk jersey, which he used for his prints. The weft, made with particularly fine fibers, was first produced by the Mabu workshop in Solbiate. Later, Pucci collaborated with Boselli, one of Como's best silk factories. The clothes in silk jersey, longer versions of his pullovers, which were made with or without sleeves and with a simple opening for the head, were immediately greeted as a promising design. Weighing less than 250 grams, the clothes could be rolled up in one hand or bundled into a suitcase without losing their impeccable folds. Spring 1960 saw the launch of "Emilioform," a fabric composed of 45 percent shantung silk and 55 percent nylon, which Pucci used for new skiing outfits that hugged the body like a second skin. The model was christened "Capsula," in homage to research carried out by NASA. Worn with flat boots inspired by Renaissance fashions, this catsuit symbolized a modern, international, and elegant style.

From the beginning of the sixties, Pucci was the jet set's favorite fashion designer. Together with his wife and muse, Cristina, the young baroness whom he married in 1959 and with whom he had two children, Alessandro and Laudomia, he formed one of the most high-profile couples in Paris, London, New York, Capri, Palm Beach, Acapulco, and Saint-Moritz. They were a perfect showcase and became a walking advertisement for the Florentine fashion house. Pucci's designs were sexy in their lightness and simplicity and, accompanied by all kinds of accessories (from handbags to umbrellas, from hats to scarves and from belts to shoes), they were regularly photographed worn by Lauren Bacall, Liz Taylor, Diana Vreeland, Audrey Hepburn, Marilyn Monroe, and Gina Lollobrigida.

a genuine admirer of femininity—who was severely contemptuous of the constraints imposed upon women by fashion—and an innovator by nature, Pucci introduced a never-ending series of small and major modifications to his designs. One significant example of this appetite for change was a contract signed in 1960 with the Chicago fashion house Formfit Rogers. Pucci designed a revolutionary collection of underwear, which he considered the essential basis upon which to show his clothes off to their best advantage. At the end of the fifties, women were still constricted by girdles that crushed the body and pushed it upwards, creating a rigid and pointed chest, to conform to the ideals of haute couture of the time. In keeping with the lighter style of his clothing, which was soft and unlined, Pucci launched the "Viva Panty," a bodysuit made from extremely fine stretch silk which neither lifted nor compressed, but instead suggested an agreeable and very natural nakedness.

After this, Pucci produced an entire range of underwear, including nightshirts characterized by their inimitable printed designs. Various other new ventures followed. In 1961 Pucci produced his first collection of porcelain tableware for Rosenthal. In 1965 he designed a complete wardrobe for the hostesses of Braniff International; in 1974 he made the "Piume" (Feathers) print for Qantas, the Australian airline. In 1969 he created his first designs for a set of bath towels, produced in the United States for Spring Mills. In the same year, he made twelve rugs, prototypes of which were later exhibited at the Museo Nacional de Arte Decorativo in Buenos Aires.

Living up to his earlier reputation, the Prince of Prints showed his profound allegiance to a period based on eclecticism, but above all on naturalness and dynamism. This was symbolized in the sixties by the thin, athletic, tanned bodies of tall, androgynous women, such as Donyale Luna, Verushka, and Edie Sedgwick. Equally important, however, were such figures as the American First Lady Jacqueline Kennedy, and such legends of cinema and show business as Brigitte Bardot, Catherine Deneuve, Jane Fonda, and Elsa Martinelli, who were photographed in outfits that emphasized the new sensual role of the body.

I n 1953 Pucci created a marvelous series of handpainted dresses. Brushstrokes representing triangles and lozenges demonstrated the influence of artists such as Mark Rothko, Robert Motherwell, and Barnett Newmann. However, the marquis never collaborated directly with the artists as Germana Maruccelli had done, for example, when creating her collection based on designs by Getulio Alviani in 1963. Pucci always worked out his designs himself. Although it is possible to identify conceptual and aesthetic similarities between his work and that of artistic currents of the time—the optical style of Bridget Riley or that of Victor Vasarely, the British pop art of Peter Blake and

Eduardo Paolozzi, the abstract Italian painting of Fausto Melotti and Lucio Fontana, of Piero Dorazio, Giuseppe Capogrossi, and Achille Perilli—Pucci always refused any direct association with modern art. His pure primary and natural colors; his taste for abstraction; his frequent choice of non-figurative forms; his modular organization of the chromatic range; and his orchestration of straight lines or curves seem instead to be inspired by the backgrounds of Renaissance paintings, or by the taste for symbolic representation and decoration found in Oriental and African cultures.

Alongside these classical and ethnic roots, Pucci's passion for speed—for the conciseness of images perceived at a distance, from a height or in movement—was particularly evident. The cult of the car, the passion for technology and scientific research and, above all, a fascination with man's capacities for invention and progression completed the profile of this neo-humanist, who was an active, rather than contemplative, party to evolution and linguistic transformation. Based on this, Pucci's patterns cannot be reduced to simply a visual dimension. They formed part of a global vision, which centered around a person who was responsible for constructing his own existence and identity in the world.

Color played a primary role. It was a signifier, an indicator of emotions, a metaphorical language that recalled the depths of the sea, iridescence, and the infinite tonalities of shadow. Journeying through the collections, one is struck by their evocative titles: "Siciliana" (1955–1956), "Palio" (1957), "Linea Modellata" (1960), "Casual Look" (1960–1961), "Romantic Lady" (1961), "Bali" (1962–1963), so many formal suggestions linked to the past or present, to ethnic or abstract places of inspiration. The creations within the collections arose from a thorough and highly sophisticated fusion of colors and forms, interpreted in all possible combinations and variations. A single glance at Pucci's tonal range reveals the results of a vast and methodical search in which color has been dissected, recomposed, and reinvented in an infinite variety of tones. Fuchsia and geranium, moon and peacock blue, lavender and banana, forest green, musk, mint green, pale green, tortoiseshell and cardinal red, sapphire and blackberry, khaki and rope, steel grey and ocean blue . . . a series of over a hundred hues and gradations.

the dominant contemporary trends in art and fashion, which sought new geometric forms capable of creating optical illusions on two-dimensional surfaces, strongly influenced Pucci's graphic experiments during the sixties. He replaced his original prints—dedicated to Cortina d'Ampezzo, to Florence and Agrigento, to the colors of Taormina and Syracuse—with stylized, modular, iterative motifs which amplified the fluidity and movement of the tones. These patterns, to which Pucci owes his fame, appeared with some regularity from July 1962 onwards, in a collection inspired by Bali. From then on, instead of drawing his inspiration from the countries of the Mediterranean, he looked to Indonesia, Africa, and South America. The idea of the "global village" of the post-Gutenberg culture captured Pucci's imagination. Impressed by Marshall McLuhan's philosophy about a multimedia society, he spent a great deal of time studying the theories of the Canadian author. The sixties were defined by unrivalled mass-media legends: the music of the Beatles, the sexual revolution, Mary Quant, the death of Marilyn Monroe, Andy Warhol's Factory, Swinging London, etc. It was, moreover, between 1962 and 1967 that Pucci enjoyed his most creative period, evidently inspired by the exciting and important interaction between fashion, design, music and science.

After the "Bali" collection it is possible to trace a new predilection for monochrome colors, combined with incredible printed motifs that are inspired by the culture of the Indonesian island. The style of the garments also became more exotic: short tunics over matching bathing suits, tubular forms printed along hemlines and long blouses tied at the waist with a sash. Trousers became sarongs, skirts that were long and knotted at the waist to reveal glimpses of the body beneath.

It was also during this period, in July 1962, that Pucci presented his first haute-couture collection. Dedicated to "Reigning Beauties," and particularly to Jacqueline Kennedy, it was typified by elongated lines designed for willowy women with narrow shoulders, small breasts, slim hips, and never-ending legs. The style of the jackets and trousers was vaguely masculine, even when complemented with a very feminine lace top. The dresses and coats were slightly flared.

During his long career, Pucci brought out four new collections a year, designing more than five hundred garments for boutiques and haute-couture lines. The constant exotic references during the sixties reflected not only his personal passion for distant locations, but also a particular interest in Asian religion and music—a fashionable tendency of the time which he knew how to appropriate and adapt with elegance. With the Autumn/Winter collection of 1964, for example, dedicated to Africa, Pucci demonstrated his negation of racism, thereby somewhat defying the American government. For the first time in fashion history, he used black models at a catwalk show at the Palazzo Pitti in Florence. African masks and idols were reinterpreted in the motifs "Naga," "Tabù," "Taitù," "Kwango," "Niger," and "Bongo."

●

In 1965, Emilio Pucci was asked to take over from Giovan Battista Giorgini as director of the Florentine shows. At the same time the Roman couturiers announced their intention to present their shows in the capital. His task was therefore not an easy one: He only had two days, a few boutiques, and five designers at his disposal (Guidi and Pucci for Florence, Fabiani for Rome, and Marucelli and Mila Schön for Milan). To raise interest among foreign clientele he developed two strategies: On the one hand he offered couture garments at reasonable prices (between 95,000 and 195,000 lire), while on the other, he sought to turn the show into a spectacular event. The "Gemini 4" project, which involved a parallel presentation, was born—the new designs for the Braniff uniform were incorporated into the framework of the haute-couture fashion show. The theme of travel was central to this show, which paid homage not only to ventures in outer space, but also to mobility and to the nomadic nature of contemporary society. Pucci designed clothing that seemed to be conceived for the future. The way the lack of gravity in space affects the movement of astronauts inspired fluid garments that highlighted the lines of the body. Sleeves were cut kimono-style, while jackets and coats of an essentially geometric nature were shaped to echo the curve of the shoulders. In contrast, the boutique collection was inspired by the costumes of medieval pages. It was a completely successful mix of the ancient and modern, articulated through the use of long and short tunics, worn over woolen tights with geometric motifs inspired by the decorated façade of the baptistery in Florence.

"Vivara," Pucci's 1966 collection, is perhaps his best known. It bears the name of the fashion house's first perfume, which had been presented in February of the same year and launched in Acapulco. The garments were cut with low V-necks, while the colors returned to the blues of the Mediterranean landscape. The prints were a highly successful combination of diagonals and floral motifs inspired by Art Nouveau. The graphic motif "Vivara" was perhaps the most successful synthesis of lines and abstract forms that Pucci created during his whole career—a motif that became a collective sign of distinction, that was reproduced on silk, cotton, towelling, plastic, and paper. It was a unique guarantee of the authenticity and provenance of clothing, scarves, beach towels, glasses, jewelry, handbags, and of the packaging of a perfume that had already achieved legendary status.

"Vivace," the 1967 Spring/Summer collection, was presented in the apartments of Pucci's palazzo (which later became the customary practice). Pajamas and bermudas, pearl embroideries and dresses and miniskirts, printed with new geometric designs, played on the clear and spectacular alternation of contrasting tones, expressing a rich range of dynamic and fluid moods. During these years, the cut of evening dresses became more revealing, producing a new silhouette that was suggestive, spectacular, and powerful, but not aggressive. This search for a new kind of refinement culminated with the Autumn/Winter 1967–1968 collection "Neo-romantica." On this occasion, Pucci launched a new fabric—cotton jersey. It was light, comfortable, and seductive. His homage to Botticelli's paintings and Aztec culture, to printed turbans and to odalisque women with small, shining helmets or spectacular hair ornaments in the form of fountains, marked the end of an era which was crowded with enthusiastic followers.

Even though they were characterized by a kind of "Puccimania," the seventies were a difficult time for the designer himself. Nineteen sixty-eight and the cultural revolution, the demonstrations, sit-ins, and the Vietnam War brought about a crisis in the fashion market. Jeans, secondhand clothes and hippie-style garments co-existed with a fashion that attempted to adapt to the era without entirely renouncing its stylistic identity. As an attentive observer of change, Pucci realized that the young were adopting positions of radical denial. He was aware of the irreversible crisis of tradition and of a crushing aversion towards the culture, choices, and tastes of the establishment. Therefore, when this wind of revolution reached Italy, he was not taken by surprise. He had already introduced changes to his designs, accommodating a vision of a future where the youth would influence, or even determine, the course of history and the evolution of aesthetics. The Spring/Summer 1971 collection "Linea Personalizzata" returned to the sporty and functional allure of the twenties. Regularly proportioned shoulders, small collars, low waists for dresses, scarves decorated with long fringes, skirts alternating with trousers for the day and evening, soft, light materials, and jersey fabrics created an image that was in keeping with street fashion. Long coats, trapezium cloaks, and dresses became a permanent feature of Pucci's look until 1976. The ease with which they could be worn was an important aspect of their success—their ample forms granted freedom of movement and interpretation to those who wore them. After 1972, Pucci's ideas were also influenced by environmental issues. With "Town and Country" (1974), he reached the peak of his expressive art. Pastel tones, floral motifs, femininity, and a folk-inspired romanticism reflected the spirit of the time.

The eighties marked the rebirth of professionalism and a return to classic, natural fibers and to an appreciation of their aesthetic qualities. It was also a return to "Made in Italy." The arrival of ready-to-wear clothing was accompanied by the new figure of the fashion designer, who signified the creative union between the manufacturer and the market. Structured garments, costly decoration, and tailoring were back in fashion. Once again, Pucci created sophisticated clothing using such materials as chiffon, organza, and crêpe and employing geometric prints in pastel tones.

h owever, the energy of the fashion world, which Pucci had depended upon, and to whose vitality he had actively contributed, began to exhaust itself. Describing himself until the end as a craftsman of fashion—"I was born a tailor, and I consider myself as such. My work is that of an artisan whose goals are quality and style"—Pucci refused to decentralize his production. Assisted by his daughter Laudomia (who took over the fashion house after his death on November 29, 1992), he transformed his company into a research laboratory. "Emilio Pucci returns" was the headline to an article by Suzy Menkes in the *International Herald Tribune*. Worn by the likes of Paloma Picasso and Isabella Rossellini, his creations made a comeback as they once again seduced the fashion world. In 1994, the prestigious exhibition "The Italian Metamorphosis," organized by Germano Celant at the Guggenheim Museum in New York, included Emilio Pucci among the photographers, architects, interior decorators, and fashion creators who were seen to represent "Made in Italy" between 1945 and 1965. In 1996, the Biennale di Firenze dedicated one of its most splendid displays to him. Today, as Laudomia explains, Emilio Pucci is represented by "two boutiques in Florence, the 'historic' boutique in New York, and sales outlets all over the world for his ready-to-wear garments and accessories. A far cry from Zermatt and Capri, they do at least guarantee that the style he created will be kept alive." A determined style which has challenged the boundaries of time and history.

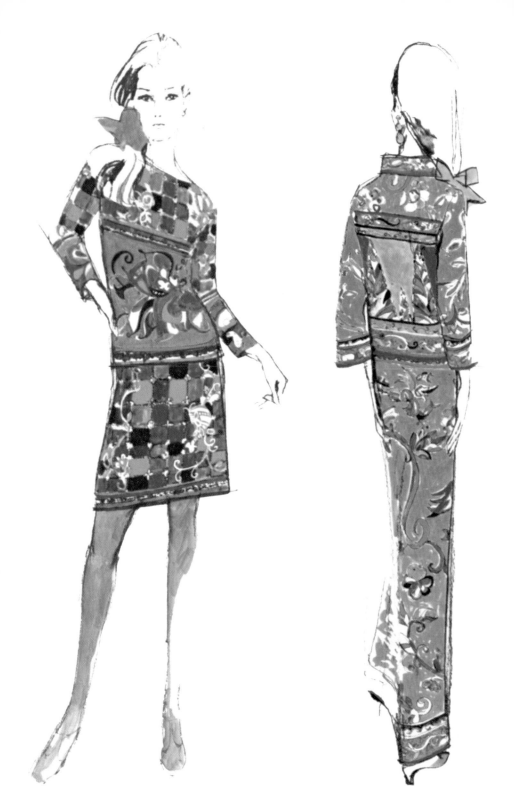

Chronology

1914   On November 20 Emilio Pucci, marquis of Barsento, is born in Naples. His parents, Orazio Pucci, and the Neapolitan countess, Augusta Pavoncelli, belong to one of the oldest Florentine families. Russian origins on his father's side.

1935–1937   Studies in the United States (Georgia and Oregon), obtaining a diploma in sociology.

1938   Joins the Italian air force as a pilot officer.

1947   Pucci shows Toni Frissell, an American photographer for *Harper's Bazaar*, his first creation, a skiing outfit. Frissell asks him to produce some models for an article on winter fashion in Europe.

1948   Toni Frissell photographs ski wear designed by Pucci. The photographs feature in the December issue of *Harper's Bazaar* and the models are sold in the big American department stores. Pucci begins his textile research: Garments in silk jersey and elasticized shantung appear from the early fifties onwards.

1949   On leave in Capri, he designs some sportswear for a friend.

1950   Pucci ends his military career. He opens La Canzone del Mare (The Song of the Sea) at Marina Piccola in Capri. Pedal pushers, straw hats, open-toed sandals, shirts with a slightly masculine cut are immediately adopted by the jet set of Capri, and then by others all around the Mediterranean. Pucci opens a workshop in his Florentine palazzo.

1951   The first Italian fashion show takes place in Florence in February, under the direction of Giovan Battista Giorgini. Pucci's fashion house presents a collection of sportswear. In July, the "Emilio" collection is greeted with enthusiasm in Florence. First meeting with Stanley Marcus, of the Neiman-Marcus department store in Dallas.

1952–1953   The launch of the "Boutique" collections. Pucci's models are sold by Saks Fifth Avenue, I. Magnin, and Bergdorf Goodman, the largest American department stores.

1954   "We owe Fashion Casuals to Marquis Emilio Pucci," announces the *New York Times* in January. Pucci receives the Neiman-Marcus Award.

1955   Pucci wins the Burdine's Sunshine Award. The "Siciliana" Autumn/Winter collection: Moorish mosaics and decorative motifs dominate abstract prints in chromatic tones.

1955–1956   The "Siciliana" Spring/Summer collection: Mediterranean influences in garments still characterized by an extreme simplicity and by technologically innovative materials. Capri pants are combined with poplin shirts printed with exclusive motifs.

1957   The "Palio" Spring/Summer collection: Chinese silks, jersey, cotton, silk twill with motifs inspired by the famous Sienese horse race.

1959   Pucci marries Cristina Nannini. Alessandro is born on December 20.

1960   Pucci signs a contract with Formfit Rogers of Chicago to design a collection of women's lingerie and nightshirts. Birth of "Viva Panty," a revolutionary stretch-silk bodysuit. Launch of "Emilioform," a fabric composed of 45 percent shantung silk and 55 percent nylon.

1960–1961   The "Casual Look" Autumn/Winter collection. As homage to NASA it included the "Capsula" model, a ski outfit made in elasticized materials.

1961   Birth of Laudomia. Pucci is the first Italian designer to receive the *Sports Illustrated* Award. The fashion press points out that his style inspired American sportswear. "Romantic Lady" Spring/Summer collection: a variety of sky-blue and lavender, black and coral, pink and burgundy shades for the "Capsula"" models and jumpsuits made in "Emilioform." The first collection of porcelain tableware for Rosenthal.

1962–1963   Pucci's first haute-couture collection, the Spring/Summer "Reigning Beauties": a homage to Jacqueline Kennedy and willowy women. The "Bali" Autumn/Winter collection, influenced by Asian and African imagination, is presented. Sarong skirts and pajama trousers with short boleros emphasize the naked body. The motifs of the prints become increasingly geometric.

Palazzo pajama evening wear with the "Zodiaco" print, including a jacket with a Nehru collar, matching turban, gold sandals, and earrings with colored stones. Photo featured in Italian Vogue, 1968. © Photo Gian Paolo Barbieri.

1963–1972	Emilio Pucci is elected as a representative of the Italian Liberal Party for the constituency of Florence/Prato/Pistoia. In Parliament, he promotes a series of acts intended to highlight the initiative and creativity of Italian workers.
1964–1965	"Cupola" Autumn/Winter collection: inspired by African colors and prints and based on the curvilinear structures of Brunelleschi's architecture.
1965	"Viva" Spring/Summer collection. Up until 1971, Pucci designs the uniforms and accessories of the air hostesses of the private Texan airline Braniff International. He takes over from Giovan Battista Giorgini as the director of the Florentine fashion shows, inviting designers to produce models at reasonable prices (95,000–195,000 lire).
1965–1966	"Gemini 4" Autumn/Winter haute-couture collection: a homage to travel. Presented at the Florentine fashion shows, it is part of a larger collection which also includes the models designed for Braniff International.
1966	"Vivara" Spring/Summer collection. "Vivara," Pucci's first perfume, is launched in Acapulco. This season's prints are the most abstract designs produced by Pucci.
1967	"Vivace" Spring/Summer collection: Bright colors and voluminous material emphasize the tropical influence of the prints. "Puccimania" begins. Mrs. Arthur A. Houghton Jr. donates her collection of Pucci clothing to the Metropolitan Museum of Art in New York. Jane Holzer, a close friend of Pucci, will later do the same.
1967–1968	"Neo-romantica" Autumn/Winter collection. Chiffon jersey is invented.
1968–1969	"Springmaid" Autumn/Winter collection for Spring Mills.
1969	"The Line is Romantic" Spring/Summer collection: exotic and folk motifs. The prints are inspired by Africa and by North American Indians, with sensual and exotic lines to provide a sense of harmony. Pucci designs twelve rugs for Dandolo y Primi in Buenos Aires, which are exhibited at the city's Museo Nacional de Arte Decorativo.
1971	"Linea Personalizzata" Spring/Summer collection: inspired by the sporting allure of the twenties. NASA commissions Pucci to design the logo for Apollo 15.
1974	The Australian airline Qantas commissions the "Piume" (Feathers) design, inspired by Australian birds and plants, from Pucci. The "Town and Country" Spring/Summer collection is presented: floral and folky in character, with light, pastel colors.
1977	Pucci designs the Lincoln Continental Mark IV for Ford.
1982	"Lady Look" Spring/Summer collection. Dedicated to Princess Diana, the collection is based on expensive materials such as organza and silk crêpe. The colors of the prints and the embroideries, which incorporate crystals and precious stones, are characterized by their pastel tones. On September 21, Pucci receives the Medal of the City of Paris from Jacques Chirac, during the first International Festival of Fashion.
1985	With his daughter Laudomia, he attends the opening of the exhibition "Italia, The Genius of Fashion," organized by the Fashion Institute of Technology in New York.
1989–1990	An economic boom brings Pucci's prints back into fashion. The fashion house reasserts its presence on the market and in the international press. Madonna, Paloma Picasso, Hamish Bowles, and Carlyne Cerf are photographed wearing Pucci clothing. Emilio retires and his daughter Laudomia begins to take over the business.
1991	On behalf of her father, Laudomia receives the Council of Fashion Designers of America Award in New York.
1992	In July, the haute-couture fashion house offers some of its most famous pieces to the costume museum in the Palazzo Pitti in Florence. Emilio Pucci dies on November 29.
1993	In spring, a Pucci boutique opens on Via della Vigna Nuova, Florence.
1994	"The Italian Metamorphosis" exhibition, curated by Germano Celant at the Guggenheim Museum, New York, includes several garments by Pucci.
1995	In spring, a Pucci boutique opens in Via Ricasoli, Florence.
1996	At the first Biennale di Firenze, a display is dedicated to the career of Emilio Pucci.

A friend of Emilio Pucci, in an extremely elegant man's skiing outfit created by the designer. Photograph featured in American Harper's Bazaar, December 1948. © Photo Toni Frissell/Emilio Pucci Archives.

Emilio Pucci

"Vivara" sculpture representing the motif of the famous design. © Emilio Pucci Archives. **Body painting on Verushka**, Emilio Pucci's star model, at the time of the launch of "Vivara" perfume in 1966. © Photo Franco Rubartelli/Emilio Pucci Archives. All rights reserved.

"Emilioform" clothing. Sapphire-blue shorts with a silk jersey top with Peruvian motifs ("Ancient Peru") and mosaic-motif shorts with a silk blouse ("Ghirigori") on the left; lavender and pale-pink trousers worn with silk blouses ("Brasilia" and "Macumba") on the right. Launched in spring 1960, "Emilioform" is a fabric composed of 45 percent shantung silk and 55 percent nylon. Used for ski wear, it is also extremely adaptable for formal dress. © Emilio Pucci Archives.

Marilyn Monroe wears a "Mirror" blouse with a pair of short, fitted shantung trousers. This photograph, taken by George Barris in the actress's home in Brentwood, made the blouse famous throughout the whole world. It was in an outfit by Pucci that Marilyn Monroe first courted Arthur Miller. © Photo George Barris.

At the **Biennale di Firenze** in September 1996, the first display was dedicated to Emilio Pucci. Two hundred embroidered silk dresses were shown on a mirrored catwalk. © Editions Assouline. **Emilio Pucci on the balcony** of his *palazzo* in Florence, with a model in a summer dress (photograph taken in 1954). His outfits are cheerful, feminine, and elegant, perfect for any occasion. © Photo Relang/Emilio Pucci Archives.

Blue, orange, and mauve printed lycra leggings, with matching velvet tunic. This photograph by Irving Penn appeared in American *Vogue* in October 1965. © Condé Nast Publications, Inc., 1965. **On the roof of Pucci's** *palazzo.* From left to right: two silk outfits with long skirts and a silk tunic and trousers in "Emilioform." This photograph by Horst appeared in *Vogue* in 1964. Courtesy of *Vogue.* © Condé Nast Publications, Inc., 1964 (renewed in 1992).

Sant'Antonio Express News (October 1966), with the "Jourdan" design. As guest of honour at the "Bella Italia" exhibition, Emilio Pucci presented his latest creations, most famously "Gemini 4," the complete line of uniforms and accessories for the air hostesses of Braniff International. © Emilio Pucci Archives/All rights reserved. **The "Orchid" design,** a chiffon negligée worn over an evening bodysuit (1966 collection). © Photo Lumachi/Emilio Pucci Archives.

Salvador Dali, a close friend of Pucci, and his wife Gala attend a private show at a Paris salon. The model wears a two-piece outfit in silk jersey, decorated with the "Airone" (Heron) design, inspired by the paintings of Henri Rousseau. © Emilio Pucci Archives/All rights reserved.

A cotton beach outfit, printed with the "Evoluzioni" design (1968), in periwinkle, turquoise and ocean blue. © Photo Alessandro Mossotti/Emilio Pucci Archives/All rights reserved.

A "Cascais" printed silk outfit with embroidery, turban, large belt, and gold Capri sandals (late 1960s–early 1970s). © Photo Gian Paolo Barbieri. **Pedal pushers in plain shantung,** with a high-necked blouse, tied at the front, and a raffia hat. The shantung was produced in Como, in pink, Veronese greens, and Neapolitan yellows. Emilio Pucci created feminine elegance in trousers. © Photo Relang/Emilio Pucci Archives.

Beach outfit in printed cotton with the "Vivara" print, one of Emilio Pucci's most famous creations. The "Vivara" line featured very simple jersey and cotton pieces with V-necks. The colors were highly original: turquoise, violet, cyclamen, orange, mint, periwinkle…. © Photo Alessandro Mossotti/Emilio Pucci Archives/All rights reserved.

Multicolored two-piece outfit in silk cashmere jersey ("Mariposa" print) and long shirt in printed orange and periwinkle silk twill. Greeting card for Christmas 1967, designed for Neiman-Marcus. © Emilio Pucci Archives. **"Moonlight" model in silk crêpe.** 1968 collection. The "Pesci" (Fishes) design was inspired by Mediterranean culture. © Photo Sandro Morricone/Emilio Pucci Archives/All rights reserved.

Emilio Pucci in one of the rooms in his *palazzo* that he used as a workshop. The collections were presented in the sumptuous setting of the ballroom. Photo by Horst, courtesy of *Vogue*. © Condé Nast Publications, Inc. 1964 (renewed in 1992). **Printed velour bags** with stained-glass patterns and leather finishings, modeled by Marisa Berenson. The bags and shoes matched the clothing. Photo Bert Stern, courtesy of *Vogue*. © Condé Nast Publications, Inc., 1965 (renewed in 1993).

Jacket with a Nehru collar in pink crêpe and an embroidered turban (1960–1970). Model in "Lance" print chiffon silk, with a chainmail-style head ornament. In the sixties, Pucci was inspired by the hippie fashion for cotton djellabas in bright colors. He created baggy trousers in gauze, gathered at the ankles, and Arab-influenced pajama trousers. Pucci paid particular attention to hairstyles. Photo featured in Italian *Vogue* in 1968. © Photos Gian Paolo Barbieri.

Bettina wearing a Pucci printed silk blouse. © All rights reserved. **Evening wear.** Spring/Summer collection 1969. The "Pesci" motif was used on thick crêpe silk, with a border decorated with precious stones. © Emilio Pucci Archives.

Emilio Pucci surrounded by his models for the launch of the perfume "Vivara" at Acapulco in February 1966. The perfume "Vivara"—whose bottle, designed by Rigaud, had geometric aquatic forms that contributed greatly to its success—was named after a deserted island near to Ischia. © Emilio Pucci Archives.

Palazzo trousers in crêpe de chine, printed with the "Cerchi" (Circles) motif. 1969 collection. © Emilio Pucci Archives. **Verushka wears a "Barracano" design** in silk crêpe with a hood and matching bikini ("Penne" [Quill] print). Spring/Summer collection 1965. A safari in Tanganyika inspired these warm colours. Photo Henry Clarke, courtesy of *Vogue*. © Condé Nast Publications, Inc., 1965 (renewed in 1993).

Sculpture inspired by details of the "Vivara" print. © Emilio Pucci Archives. "Odalisca" evening outfit in shantung, with turban, large belt and Capri silver-coloured sandals (late 1960s). © Photo Gian Paolo Barbieri.

Bathroom decor inspired by Emilio Pucci's sketches for the "Spring Mills" line, published in the *Los Angeles Times* (27 September 1967). Pucci produced many creations for Spring Mills: towels, curtains, cushions…. © Emilio Pucci Archives/ All rights reserved. **Long dress in silk jersey,** printed with the "Quadratini" (Checks) motif in black, dark brown and turquoise. Autumn/Winter collection 1997. © Photo Lucio Gelsi/Emilio Pucci Archives/All rights reserved.

"Vivara" fabric from the beachwear line. © Emilio Pucci Archives. **Two-piece bathing suit** in lycra, printed with the "Oroscopo" (Horoscope) motif, in fuchsia, black and mustard yellow. Spring/Summer collection 1992. Photo featured in Italian *Vogue*, June 1992. © Photo Walter Chin.

Jersey silk top, printed with the "Manis" motif (1963). © Emilio Pucci Archives. Jersey silk printed tunic. Spring/Summer collection 1996. © Photo Sathoshi Saikusa/French *Vogue*, May 1996.

Isabella Rossellini wears a silk jersey "Vivara" top. Photo featured in Italian *Vogue*, September 1990. © Photo Steven Meisel. **Piper's Girl.** The singer Patty Bravo, of great fame in Italy, is a faithful follower of Pucci's style. Here she wears a short silk jersey dress, with the "Cactus" motif. In ocean blue and pale pink, it was very fashionable during the sixties. © OGGI/RCS Periodici.

Silk jersey dress, with the "Giardino" (Garden) print. © Photo Franco Rubartelli/ French *Vogue*, June–July 1969. **Isabella Rossellini wears a "Vivara" Pucci print.** Photo featured in Italian *Vogue* in 1990. © Photo Steven Meisel.

Emilio Pucci and his daughter Laudomia (embroidered dress and jacket by Pucci), at the exhibition "Italia, The Genius of Fashion," organized in 1985 by the Fashion Institute of Technology in New York. © Courtesy Georgianna Appignani/Emilio Pucci Archives. **Fabrics created for the "Fantasioso" collection** in 1963. This photo by Horst featured in American *Vogue* in March 1964. Courtesy of *Vogue*. © Condé Nast Publications, Inc., 1964 (renewed in 1992).

Cotton gabardine printed skirt in orange, yellow, and apple green. Spring/Summer collection 1997. The "Giungla" (Jungle) design has wide borders. © *Palm Beach Magazine*/All rights reserved. **Silk twill blouse printed with the "Festa" (Party) motif,** worn by the model Paula Ospina with velour stretch trousers. Autumn/Winter collection 1997. © Photo Lucio Gelsi/Emilio Pucci Archives.

Bibliography

G. Celant (ed.), *Identité italienne. L'Art en Italie depuis* 1959, Centre Georges Pompidou and Centro di Firenze, 1981

G. Celant (ed.), *The Italian Metamorphosis* 1943–1968, The Guggenheim Museum, New York, 1994

M. L. Frisa, "The Air Around Us," in *Emilio Pucci, Biennale di Firenze,* Skira, 1996

K. le Bourhis, "Emilio Pucci: an American Success 1948–1992: the Socio-cultural and Fashion Context of Pucci Rise and Triumph in the United States," in *Emilio Pucci, Biennale di Firenze,* Skira, 1996

S. Ricci, "Emilio Pucci: a Stylistic Path," in *Emilio Pucci, Biennale di Firenze,* Skira, 1996

L. Settembrini, "Lessons at the Sherry Netherland," in *Emilio Pucci, Biennale di Firenze,* Skira, 1996

G. Uzzani, "Parallel Paths," in *Emilio Pucci, Biennale di Firenze,* Skira, 1996

M. Casadio, *Conversazione con Laudomia Pucci,* March 1998 (unpublished)

E. Mannucci, *Il Marchese rampante. Emilio Pucci: avventure, illusioni, successi di un inventore della moda italiana,* Baldini & Castoldi, Florence, 1998

Acknowledgments

The Publishers would like to thank the Emilio Pucci fashion house, and particularly Laudomia Pucci and Francesca Tosi, for their assistance in preparing this work.

Thanks are also due to the photographers Gian Paolo Barbieri, George Barris, Walter Chin, Lucio Gelsi, Steven Meisel, Irving Penn, and Sathoshi Saikusa; as well as to the models Bettina, Isabella Rossellini, and Verushka.

Finally, this work would not have been possible without the kind assistance of Angela Carbonetti (William Morris Agency), Michael Costa (Marek & Associates), Lisa Diaz (American *Vogue*), Nathalie (Marilyn Agency), Thierry Le Saux and Thomas Bonnouvrier (Side Winder), Sonia Paitori (RCS), Rosanna Sguera (Art & Commerce Anthology), Angela Weigand (*Hamptons Magazine*), and Michèle Zaquin (French *Vogue*).